Moving and growing

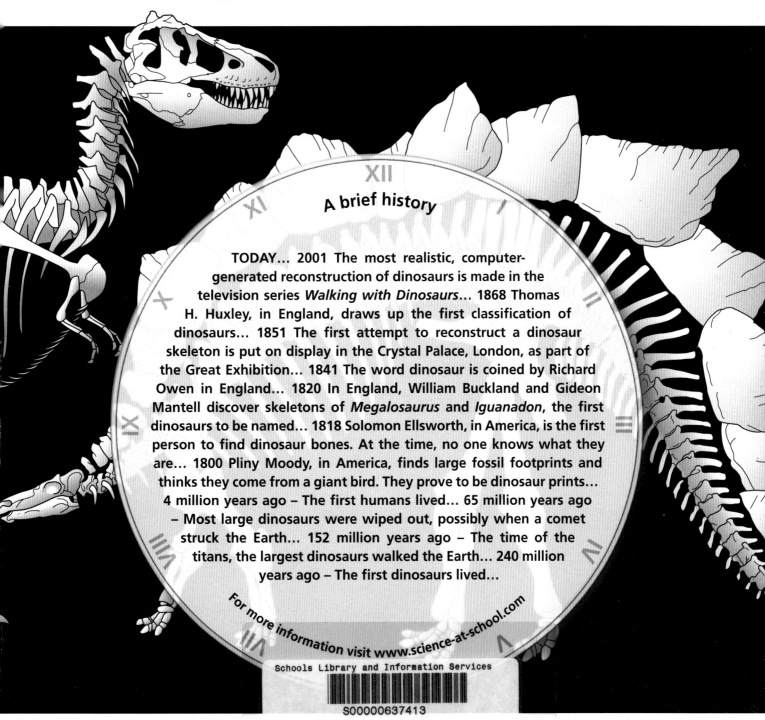

A brief history

TODAY... 2001 The most realistic, computer-generated reconstruction of dinosaurs is made in the television series *Walking with Dinosaurs*... 1868 Thomas H. Huxley, in England, draws up the first classification of dinosaurs... 1851 The first attempt to reconstruct a dinosaur skeleton is put on display in the Crystal Palace, London, as part of the Great Exhibition... 1841 The word dinosaur is coined by Richard Owen in England... 1820 In England, William Buckland and Gideon Mantell discover skeletons of *Megalosaurus* and *Iguanadon*, the first dinosaurs to be named... 1818 Solomon Ellsworth, in America, is the first person to find dinosaur bones. At the time, no one knows what they are... 1800 Pliny Moody, in America, finds large fossil footprints and thinks they come from a giant bird. They prove to be dinosaur prints... 4 million years ago – The first humans lived... 65 million years ago – Most large dinosaurs were wiped out, possibly when a comet struck the Earth... 152 million years ago – The time of the titans, the largest dinosaurs walked the Earth... 240 million years ago – The first dinosaurs lived...

For more information visit www.science-at-school.com

Dr Brian Knapp

Word list

These are some science words that you should look out for as you go through the book. They are shown using CAPITAL letters.

BONE
A hard material that looks like stone but is really alive. Bones grow and can repair themselves when broken. Bones also contain marrow, a source of new blood for the body.

BRITTLE
A material that does not bend easily when a force is applied to it, but instead tends to snap.

CARTILAGE
A sheet of padding between bones. It is found in all joints and stops the bones from scraping against one another as they move.

CLAM
A water-living animal with two shells.

CLOT
A place where blood cells have collected together into a hardened mass.

DINOSAUR
A group of land-living reptiles that lived between about 240 million and 65 million years ago.

Dinosaurs were all shapes and sizes, but did not include sea-living or flying reptiles.

ENERGY
The ability to do work.

JOINT
The place where two bones come together and are connected by ligament. Joints allow movement.

LIGAMENT
Strong fibres that connect bones to other bones across a joint.

MARROW
Soft, jelly-like tissue that fills the inside of the bones. New blood cells for the body are made in the marrow.

MOLLUSC
A type of soft-bodied animal with a shell, a head and a muscular 'foot' for digging. They usually live in water. Clams are molluscs.

MOULT
To shed one skin, or shell, and grow another, larger one.

MUSCLE
Strong, fibre-like flesh that can shorten when it receives a signal from the brain. Muscles allow us to move by pulling across the joints in our skeleton. The more weight a muscle needs to move, the bigger it is. The biggest muscles are in the upper legs and buttocks.

NERVE
Long cells that connect the brain to different parts of the body. Electrical signals are sent along the nerves to control how the body works.

SHELL
A hard casing that is used to support and protect some animals, such as clams.

SKELETON
The framework of bones that gives you shape.

SKULL
The hollow ball of bone that protects the brain.

Contents

Weblink: www.science-at-school.com

The skeleton inside you

The shape of your body is formed by the skeleton inside you.

Most of us have seen pictures of **SKELETONS**. But what does the skeleton inside you look like?

Your body is a collection of **BONES** (Picture 1). There are over 200 bones in your body. A baby has 275 bones, but by the time you are grown up, 69 bones will have joined together so that you will have only 206.

Skeletons are frames

We need a skeleton to hold up all of our soft parts, just like a building needs a frame to hold up its walls and floors. Our frame happens to be inside us and so we don't normally see it (Picture 2). Our skeleton is covered by **MUSCLE** and skin, so we are soft to touch. But a bony frame is not the only kind of skeleton. Some animals have liquid skeletons, and others have their skeletons on the outside, often in the form of **SHELLS** (as you will see on pages 22 to 23). These animals look very different from us. While those animals with liquid skeletons (like worms) are soft and squidgy to touch, those with outside skeletons are mainly hard to touch. If we had hard shells, they might look like suits of armour.

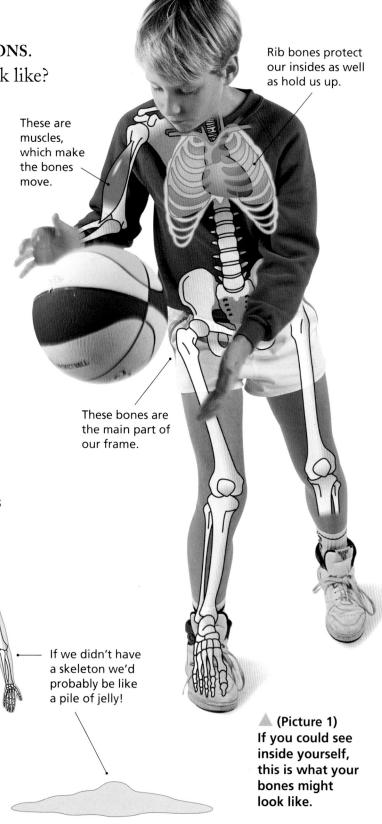

These are muscles, which make the bones move.

Rib bones protect our insides as well as hold us up.

These bones are the main part of our frame.

If we didn't have a skeleton we'd probably be like a pile of jelly!

▲ (Picture 1) If you could see inside yourself, this is what your bones might look like.

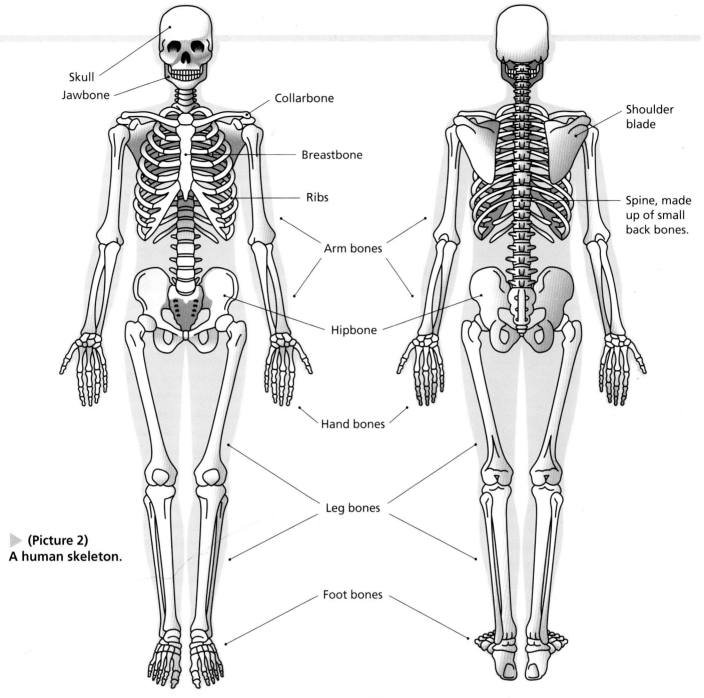

Skull

Jawbone

Collarbone

Breastbone

Ribs

Arm bones

Hipbone

Hand bones

Leg bones

Foot bones

Shoulder blade

Spine, made up of small back bones.

▶ (Picture 2)
A human skeleton.

Inside skeletons move

Your bones are not all stuck together rigidly. Instead, they are held together in such a way that they can move. The parts of your body that move the skeleton are called muscles. Bones are connected together at **JOINTS**. Here, the bones are often not stuck together, but are held together loosely so they can move.

Bones protect

Some bones do more than just hold us up. Their strength also means that bones can protect delicate parts of our bodies, such as our brain, lungs and heart.

Summary
- Bones make a frame which supports soft body parts.
- Bones protect delicate parts of the body.
- Bones can be moved about.

5

Head and back bones

Your spine carries the weight of your head and all of your upper body.

Each of your bones is shaped to do a special job. Bones that do not carry a lot of weight are thinner, and often flatter, than those that carry large weights. The further down your body you go, the more weight the bones are carrying. This is why the sturdiest bones are in the lower half of your body.

Head bones

The eight bones in your head fit together like a jigsaw puzzle and form the main part of your **SKULL**. These bones are thin and plate-like (Picture 1) and protect your brain. Your face is made up from 20 more bones.

Back bones

If the bones in your back fitted together like a jigsaw, you would not be able to move. Instead, most of the 33 bones in your back fit together to allow your body to move (Picture 2). However, they must also carry a lot of weight, not just from your arms, but also from your upper body in general. As a result, the bones of the spine mostly get bigger towards the bottom (the bottom nine bones are joined together).

Having a lot of bones in your back allows you to bend and twist in many more ways than if you just had one or two back bones.

At the top of your back is a special bone that allows your head to twist from side to side.

All of the other bones are shaped like little pillars. They are separated from one another by discs of a jelly-like material. These act like cushions, keeping the back bones from rubbing together.

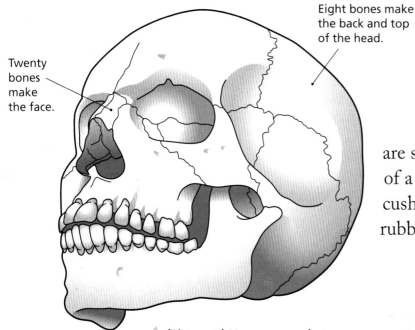

Twenty bones make the face.

Eight bones make the back and top of the head.

(Picture 1) You can see that your head bones fit together like plates that have been zippered together. There are holes for eyes, nose and so on.

Summary

- The bones in your skull are fixed together to protect your brain.
- Your back bones can move.
- Back bones are kept apart by soft discs.

Weblink: www.science-at-school.com

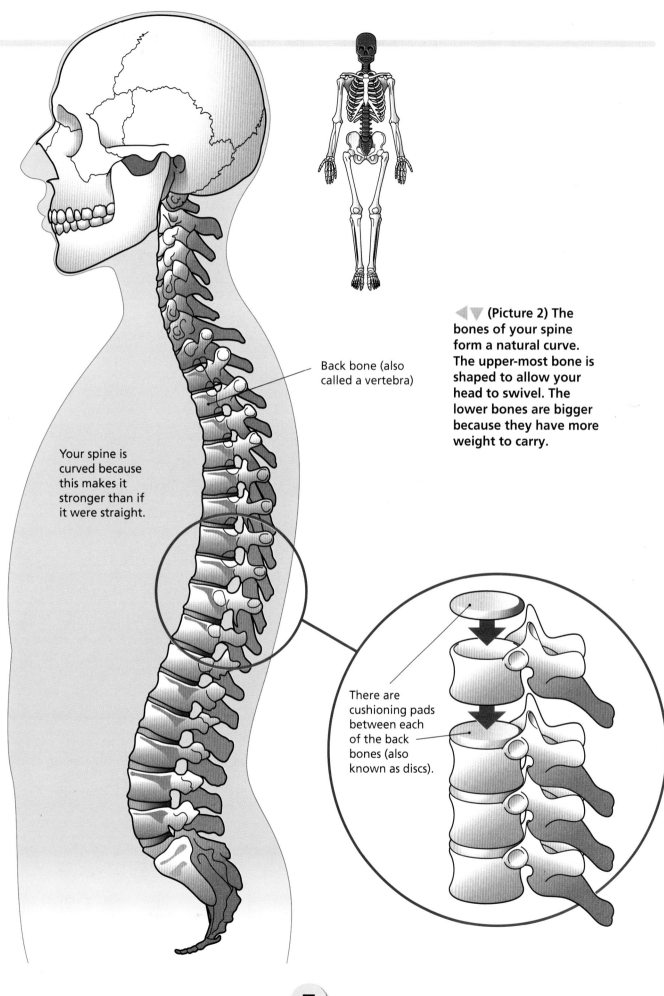

Back bone (also called a vertebra)

Your spine is curved because this makes it stronger than if it were straight.

(Picture 2) The bones of your spine form a natural curve. The upper-most bone is shaped to allow your head to swivel. The lower bones are bigger because they have more weight to carry.

There are cushioning pads between each of the back bones (also known as discs).

7

Arm and leg bones

Arms and legs are strong tubes of bone. The ends of each bone are shaped to allow them to move.

The arms, legs, hands and feet are mostly made of long, thin, tubular bones with nobbly ends. In between the long bones are pebble-shaped bones (for example in your wrists). This arrangement gives you the chance to move your arms and legs in an amazing number of ways.

▼ (Picture 1) The ball-and-socket joint at the top of the upper leg bone (thighbone) allows the leg to turn in many directions.

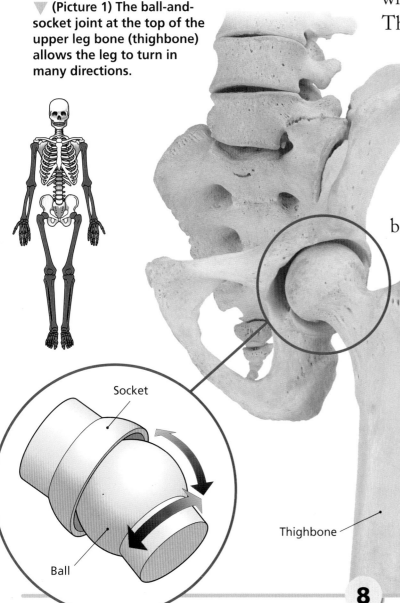

Socket

Ball

Thighbone

Arms and legs

Arms and legs are each made of three bones: one in the upper half of the limb and two in the lower half.

If they were solid, these bones would be extremely heavy. They would also be more **BRITTLE** and liable to break. Instead, they are in the form of tubes, which makes them lighter and stronger. The inside of the bones is not hollow. It contains a substance called **MARROW**, which makes blood for the body.

The upper ends of the upper arm and leg bones are shaped like round balls. The arm bones fit into cup-shaped hollows in the collar bones, and the leg bones fit into a broad hipbone called the pelvis. Being ball-shaped at the ends allows the arm and leg bones to move in many directions (Picture 1).

The other ends of the arm and leg bones (at your knees, feet, hands and elbows) are not ball-shaped (Picture 2). These bones only move in one direction. If these bones also had ball-shaped ends it would be much harder to control how your arms and legs moved.

This ball-shaped joint allows movement in any direction.

Joint only moves in one direction

The shape of this joint allows movement mainly in just one direction.

Hands and feet

Your hands and feet are made of many small bones (Picture 3). This gives them enormous flexibility. Again, some have straight joints and others more rounded joints. Just as in the arms and legs, this combination of joints allows you to keep easy control of your movements.

Wrist bones

(Picture 3) Most of the bones in the hand can only move in one direction. A large number of small bones in the wrist give it the most flexible movement.

Finger bones

Summary

- Arms and legs are made up of long, tubular bones.
- The ends of the bones are shaped to allow one bone to move against another.

Living bones

Bones are made up of a living material, just like any other part of your body. This is how they can repair themselves when they break.

Although bones may appear to be lifeless, they are in fact made of living material just like the rest of the body. Because it is alive, bone can grow and repair itself if it gets broken. If bones were dead they would not be able to do this.

The ends of the long bones contain a red material called marrow (Picture 1). This is where fresh blood is made for our bodies. Fresh blood leaves the marrow and travels through the bone in tiny tubes which connect to the rest of our blood.

Hollow bones

Bones are made of a heavy, strong material. However, bone is not solid, but like a honeycomb. This keeps it strong, but also as light as possible.

Bones are made using a substance called calcium. Bones cannot grow without it. That is why the food we eat and drink must contain enough calcium to build strong bones. Milk, for example, is rich in calcium. So are many fruits.

Holding bones together

Bones support us through their strength and rigidity. Joints

▼ (Picture 1)
Inside a bone.

Each end of the bone is shaped to connect with other bones. The bone spreads out and is bulbous. This has two uses: the bulbous end gives a large surface for the muscles to attach to; and it provides a large surface to form a joint. A large bone joint may be less flexible but it is less likely to be pushed out of place.

The bone ends are made of spongy bone, whose honeycombed spaces are filled with red marrow.

Hard bone under surface 'skin'.

The shaft of long bones is filled with fatty yellow marrow in adults and with red marrow in growing children.

The surface of the bone is covered with a white layer of fibres, a kind of 'skin'. This provides a good surface for muscles to attach to.

Weblink: www.science-at-school.com

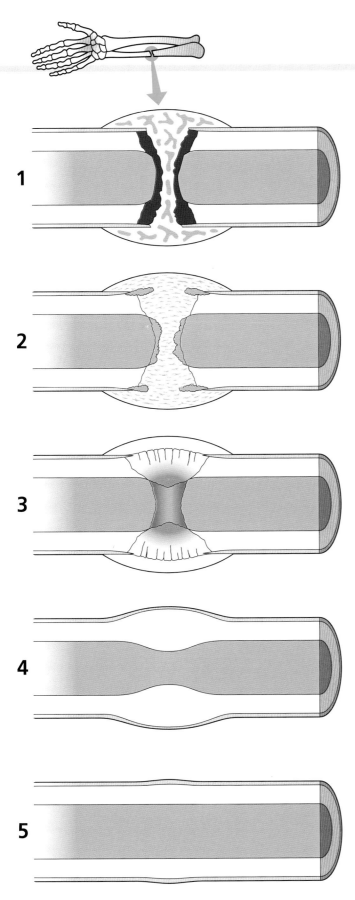

help the bones move. Joints have special cushions – called **CARTILAGE**, to help them move smoothly. Bones and cartilage are 'lashed' together by strong, rubbery fibres called **LIGAMENT**.

By themselves, bones, cartilage and ligaments cannot make us move. For this we use flesh called muscle. You will find out more about muscles on pages 14 to 15.

When bones break

For all their strength, bones are brittle and cannot bend. This makes them likely to break if a large force acts on them, such as in an accident.

When a bone breaks, the blood vessels running through it break too, causing bleeding and swelling (Picture 2). The blood then **CLOTS**, forming a temporary kind of glue until the bone has repaired itself. This clotted blood makes the area around the bone swell.

After about one week, bone cells from the broken ends start to grow into the clotted area. It takes months for the bone ends to knit together properly, and in the meantime the bone is weak and there is a risk of further breakage. This is why broken bones are supported with plaster casts.

▲ Bone repair. (1) Swelling occurs because blood clots around the break. (2) A week later new bone starts to grow. (3) After three weeks, the broken ends grow together. (4) The repaired bone is thicker because it has new bone as well as old bone. (5) After several months, the bone returns to its original thickness.

Summary

- Bones are made up of living material as are all other parts of the body.
- Bones are made using calcium.
- Bones repair themselves when they are broken.

Weblink: www.science-at-school.com

Bones grow

Your bones are not made of unchanging material, but grow and change shape throughout your life.

If you look at pictures of yourself when you were a baby and compare them with pictures of you now, you will see many changes (Picture 1). You are much bigger than you were, but you are also a different shape. This is because of the way that your bones grow.

Live bones grow

When you are born, some of your bones are not even formed, but are made of soft material called cartilage. This is one reason babies have to be handled with care (Picture 2).

Aged under 1   Aged about 11

▲ (Picture 1) As you grow bigger, your face grows longer at a faster rate than it grows wider. This is why babies have rounder faces than adults.

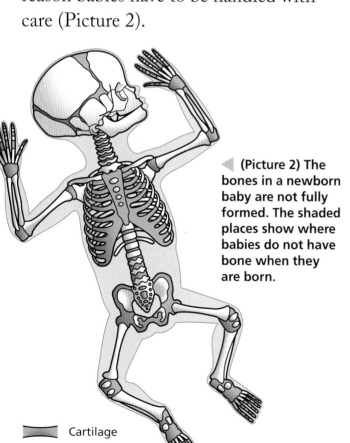

◄ (Picture 2) The bones in a newborn baby are not fully formed. The shaded places show where babies do not have bone when they are born.

▬ Cartilage

▬ Bone

Weblink: www.science-at-school.com

Bones mainly grow at their ends. This is why you grow much taller than wider (Picture 3). Of course, your bones also grow thicker. If they did not, they would be too thin and liable to break.

Old bones change

Even once you have grown up your bones do not stop changing. In fact, your bones will continue changing throughout your life. Until the age of about 35, people add more new bone than is needed to replace old bone. As a result, they tend to get bigger. After this, they may begin to lose more bone than they grow. This is why some old people become smaller and why their bones become thinner and more liable to break.

Summary

- Bones continue to grow throughout your life.
- Bones grow bigger until middle age. Then they stop, and finally get smaller.

(Picture 3) As you grow you get much taller than wider.

Average height of eleven year olds.

Average height of eight year olds.

Average height of six year olds.

Weblink: www.science-at-school.com

Muscles move bones

Bones have rounded ends so they can be moved. But to move them requires muscles.

As we have seen, your bones form the scaffolding on which every other part of you hangs. However, the bones are just part of the story, for on their own they cannot make you move. For this you need muscles. Muscles are soft parts of the body (flesh) that can change shape to pull your bones into new positions.

Arm muscles

Back muscles

Buttock muscles hold the pelvis.

Upper leg muscles

▶ (Picture 1) Most of the bulk of the leg is made from muscle.

Lower leg muscles

A body filled with muscles

There are over 600 muscles in your body. Most of the bones are surrounded by muscles. The muscles fill out your body and are covered in a thin layer of skin. The muscles help you to move, and the skin protects all of the insides of your body.

Some muscles need to be strong and so these muscles are large. The muscles in your legs are like this because they need to move your whole body (Picture 1). The muscles in your arms do not carry much weight and so they are lighter. The lightweight bones and smaller muscles explains why your arms are more slender than your legs.

How muscles work

Muscles can only tighten or relax, they cannot push. Muscles become shorter when they tighten, and they become longer when they relax.

Muscles always work in pairs, one each side of a joint. This is why every joint in your body has at least two muscles. Most joints, however, are worked by groups of muscles.

When you are not moving, the muscles each side of a joint are both pulling by the same amount and nothing happens. When you want to move, your brain tells one of the muscles to tighten and shorten, while it tells the other to relax and lengthen.

Weblink: www.science-at-school.com

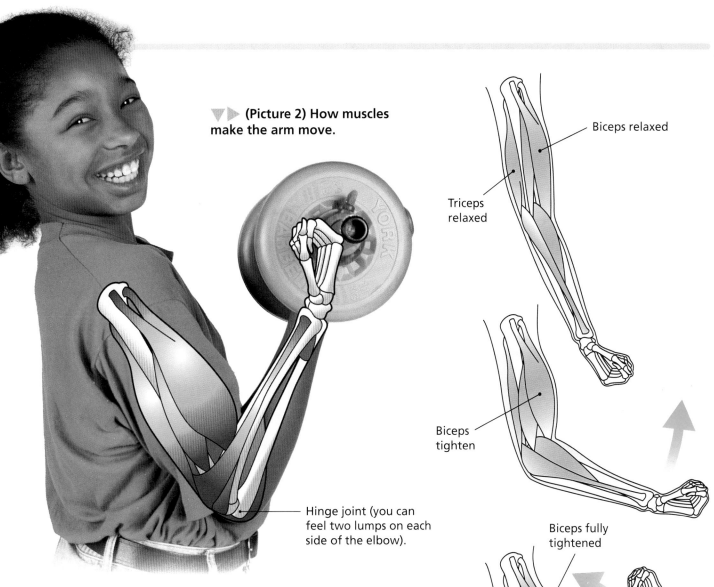

(Picture 2) How muscles make the arm move.

Biceps relaxed

Triceps relaxed

Hinge joint (you can feel two lumps on each side of the elbow).

Biceps tighten

Biceps fully tightened

Triceps relaxed

Biceps relax

Triceps tighten

Muscles while we sleep

Muscles can never stop pulling while you are awake. If they did, your bones would not be held together properly and your body would lose its shape! Many muscles do relax, however, when we sleep, so then the body needs support. That is why we cannot sleep standing up.

Summary

- Most bones are surrounded by muscles.
- Muscles work in groups.
- Muscles cause movement by tightening and relaxing.

Weblink: www.science-at-school.com

Muscles use electricity and energy

Muscles can only move because they get electrical instructions and a continuous supply of energy.

You have seen how we are held up by a kind of scaffolding called a skeleton, and how the skeleton is moved by muscles. But the muscles can only move if they are told to do so by the brain, and if they have enough **ENERGY**.

Signals from the brain

In a very famous scientific experiment in 1786, an Italian scientist named Luigi Galvani made a dead frog's leg twitch by connecting the muscles between two pieces of metal.

By accident, Galvani had made a battery using the two pieces of metal, and this battery then sent an electric current down the frog's leg. This current is what caused the leg to twitch.

Galvani had discovered that muscles receive signals of electricity.

We now know that all muscles are controlled by tiny electrical signals. The signals are sent from the brain along tiny fibres called **NERVES** (Picture 1).

When we want to raise our arm, for example, the brain sends a tiny electric signal down the nerve leading to the muscle called the biceps. This causes the biceps to shorten and the arm is lifted (Picture 2).

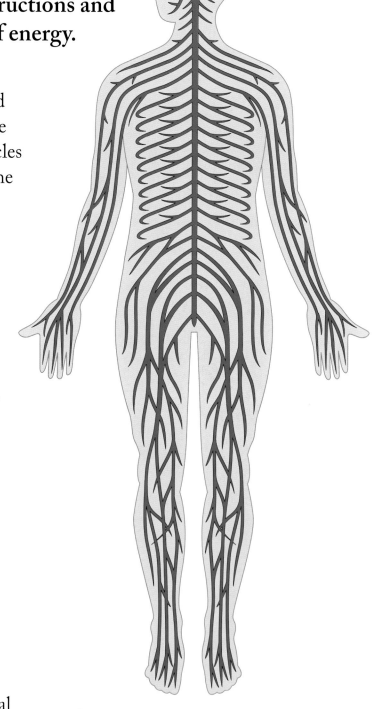

▲ **(Picture 1) The brain is constantly taking in information from your senses and sending instructions to your body on how to respond. It does this using millions of tiny electrical signals that pass up and down your nerves.**

Weblink: www.science-at-school.com

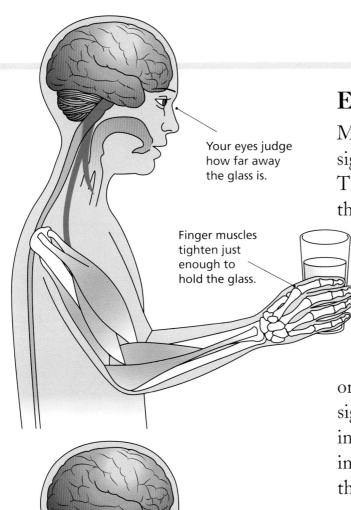

Your eyes judge how far away the glass is.

Finger muscles tighten just enough to hold the glass.

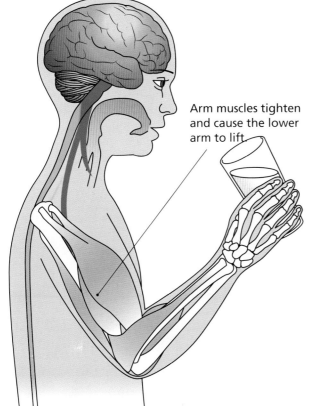

Arm muscles tighten and cause the lower arm to lift

(Picture 2) In order to perform even a simple action, such as holding a glass of water, your brain must constantly send signals between the muscles in your fingers, hand, arm and eyes. These signals must all work together to allow you to hold the glass.

Energy and oxygen from blood

Muscles move because of electrical signals, but they also need energy. This is brought to the muscles through the blood.

The blood carries a great variety of chemicals that have been extracted from the food we eat. It also carries oxygen. Some of the chemicals in the blood are a useful source of energy. Sugar is one of these. When the brain sends a signal to a muscle, the oxygen and sugar in the blood change the stored energy in the sugar into movement energy for the muscle.

Every time the brain signals the muscle to move, some energy is used up. If we move for a long time, we may use up all of the spare energy in the muscle. When this happens, we feel tired and may even get cramps. That is why we have to slow down or stop moving to let the blood bring new chemicals and oxygen to the muscles.

People who exercise regularly have more stored energy and oxygen in their muscles, so they can move quickly for longer without feeling tired.

Summary
- Muscles move when they receive electrical signals from the brain.
- Muscles need energy and oxygen to work.
- When we have used up the oxygen and energy stored in the muscles we feel tired and slow down.

Weblink: www.science-at-school.com

Animal bones

Animal bones are shaped differently because animals move differently.

Our bones are designed for the way we live. Other animals live quite differently, and so you should not be surprised to find that their bones are very different too.

Bird bones

Try flapping your arms and you will not take off. This is not just because you do not have wings: it is also because you are too heavy to fly. Your bones are designed for taking your weight on the ground. If you look at the bones of a bird, you will see that they are lightweight, thinner and hollow. They are designed for flying (Pictures 1 and 2).

Birds also have enormously long arms compared to us. Their arm bones are connected together inside their bodies with tendons, whereas our arms are set far apart so they can work separately.

Wishbone

Upper wing bone

This large breast muscle pulls the wing up.

The breastbone in birds is very large to withstand the forces of the muscles that act on it.

This large and powerful breast muscle pulls the wing down.

Human bone is heavy. Bird bones are thin and hollow, which makes them very light. Supporting struts keep them from collapsing.

◀◀▲ (Picture 1) These pictures show a bird skeleton. Look closely at the upper wing bone which has been partly cut away to show the inside. The bone is very thin and lightweight.

(Picture 2) The bones in bird wings are designed to work together so the bird can fly.

Frog bones

The frog is another animal with bones shaped very differently from ours. Frogs have enormously long legs with powerful muscles. The legs are normally folded up, but they can straighten instantly, causing the frog to spring away from danger (Picture 3).

With leg bones of this shape, frogs never walk: they can only hop.

Summary

- Birds have long 'arm' bones which they use as wings.
- Bird bones are very lightweight.
- Frogs have very long hind leg bones to allow them to spring away from danger.

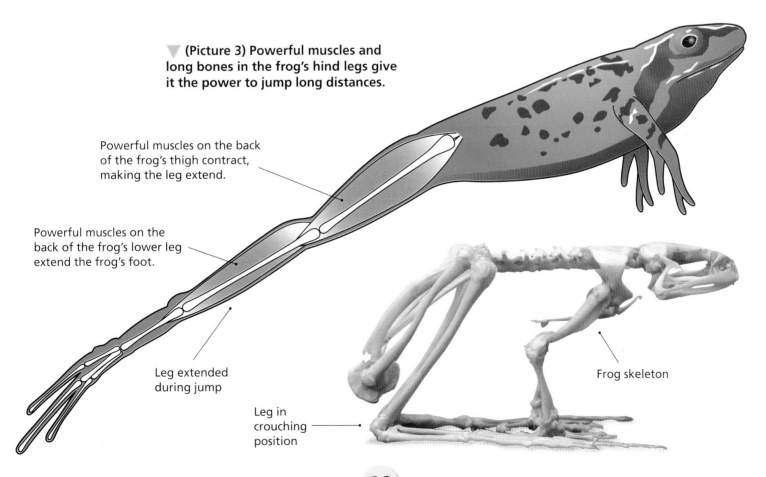

(Picture 3) Powerful muscles and long bones in the frog's hind legs give it the power to jump long distances.

Powerful muscles on the back of the frog's thigh contract, making the leg extend.

Powerful muscles on the back of the frog's lower leg extend the frog's foot.

Leg extended during jump

Leg in crouching position

Frog skeleton

Weblink: www.science-at-school.com

Dinosaurs

The world's biggest creatures came in all shapes and sizes, but we can use their skeletons to suggest how they lived.

The **DINOSAURS**, which were ancient reptiles that lived on land, were the largest creatures ever to live on the planet. But as they died out 65 million years ago, no one has ever seen a dinosaur. However, from studying their bones, we know much about how they lived, what they looked like and how they moved.

Modern reptiles are not descended from dinosaurs, so looking at modern reptiles is of limited help. Scientists are not even sure whether dinosaurs were warm- or cold-blooded. Evidence now suggests they were warm-blooded, whereas modern reptiles are cold-blooded.

Dinosaur size and speed

Some of the biggest dinosaurs were tens of metres long, over ten metres tall and weighed tens of tonnes.

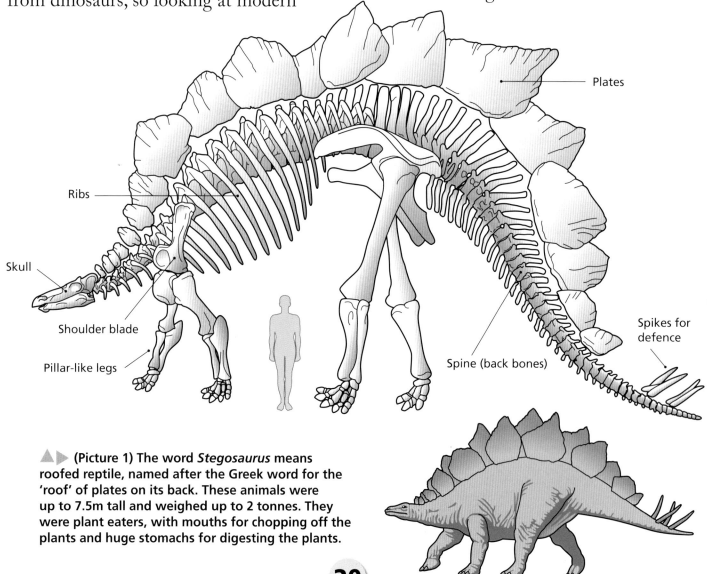

▲▶ **(Picture 1)** The word *Stegosaurus* means roofed reptile, named after the Greek word for the 'roof' of plates on its back. These animals were up to 7.5m tall and weighed up to 2 tonnes. They were plant eaters, with mouths for chopping off the plants and huge stomachs for digesting the plants.

Weblink: www.science-at-school.com

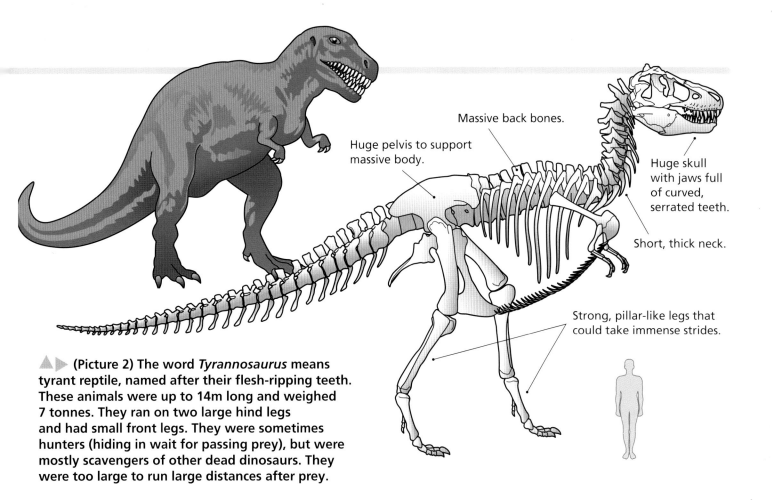

Massive back bones.

Huge pelvis to support massive body.

Huge skull with jaws full of curved, serrated teeth.

Short, thick neck.

Strong, pillar-like legs that could take immense strides.

(Picture 2) The word *Tyrannosaurus* means tyrant reptile, named after their flesh-ripping teeth. These animals were up to 14m long and weighed 7 tonnes. They ran on two large hind legs and had small front legs. They were sometimes hunters (hiding in wait for passing prey), but were mostly scavengers of other dead dinosaurs. They were too large to run large distances after prey.

Animals of this size could not move quickly, and so the biggest dinosaurs, such as *Stegosaurus* (Picture 1), could not have hunted for food. Instead, they had to be plant eaters. They had teeth suited to tearing at leaves, and huge stomachs to digest the tonnes of food they ate.

The smaller dinosaurs were lighter and so were able to move more quickly. These were the meat eaters, of which *Tyrannosaurus* (Picture 2) is one of the largest, with a huge head and flesh-ripping teeth, although *Deinonychus* (a wolf-sized animal) was probably the most ferocious, especially because it hunted in packs.

Special features

The legs of dinosaurs were tucked in under their bodies, rather than sticking out at the sides like other reptiles. This is what allowed them to move quickly and, for some, to stand on two legs. Many of the hunting dinosaurs, like *Tyrannosaurus*, walked on two legs. As a result, their arm bones are much thinner than their leg bones. The large plant eaters walked on all fours, and so their legs are similar in size.

A few dinosaurs had special plates on their backs. *Stegosaurus* had a double row of giant plates down its back, possibly to support skin and to act like radiators, getting rid of excess heat.

Summary
- Many dinosaurs were large and so needed large bones to support them.
- The hunting dinosaurs were mainly two-legged.
- The plant-eating dinosaurs needed large bodies to digest the food they ate.

Weblink: www.science-at-school.com

Animals without bones

Most of the world's animals do not have bones, but instead have either skeletons on the outside (such as insects) or skeletons made of liquid (such as worms).

Many animals do not have a skeleton inside their body. Some animals do not even have a hard skeleton at all.

Worms and leaches

Animals such as worms and leaches have a watery skeleton, something like a balloon filled with water (Picture 1). These animals need to live in moist conditions, otherwise they will dry out and go limp.

Insects, crabs and clams

Another kind of skeleton is found on the outside of the animal. In this case, the skeleton forms a hard, protective case. The muscles are attached to the inside of the skeleton and pull against one another over joints to make the animal move (Picture 2).

An insect flies by changing the shape of its skeleton where the wings are attached. One set of muscles pulls the skeleton down so that the wings go up, and the other set pulls the skeleton up so that the wings are forced down.

Many sea-living animals, such as crabs, prawns and lobsters, also have an outside skeleton called a shell (Picture 3).

Another group of animals with shells are snails, mussels, oysters and **CLAMS**. Together they are often called **MOLLUSCS** (Picture 4).

Some molluscs move by opening and shutting their shells quickly. This forces out the water and pushes them along.

▼ **(Picture 1) What the inside of a worm looks like.**

The worm is surrounded by a 'tube' of strong muscles that press in to move the worm forward.

The inside of the worm is mostly filled with a watery jelly.

The worm is split up into segments, or compartments.

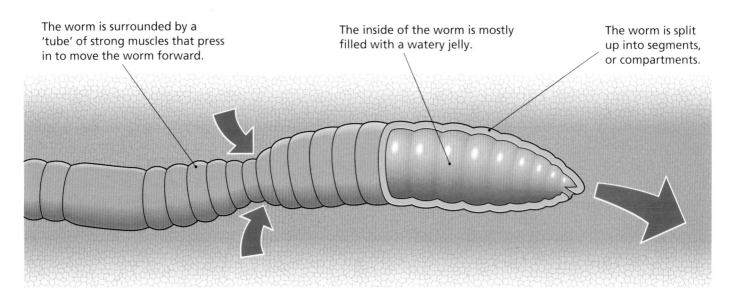

Weblink: www.science-at-school.com

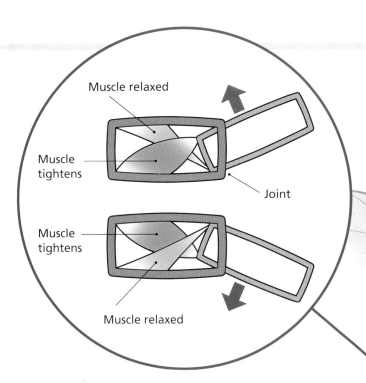

Muscle relaxed

Muscle tightens

Joint

Muscle tightens

Muscle relaxed

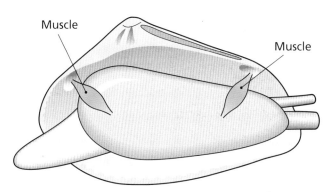

(Picture 2) Insects have a hard, rigid skeleton on the outside. Sections of the skeleton are connected at joints and moved by muscles on the inside.

How shelled animals grow

Some shells change size and grow with the animal. Clam shells are like this. However, for insects, crabs and lobsters, living in a shell is like living in a suit of armour. The animal might grow, but the shell does not. As a result, from time to time the animal has to squeeze out of its shell and then quickly grow another, bigger one. This is called **MOULTING**.

▼ (Picture 3) The shell of a crab is its skeleton.

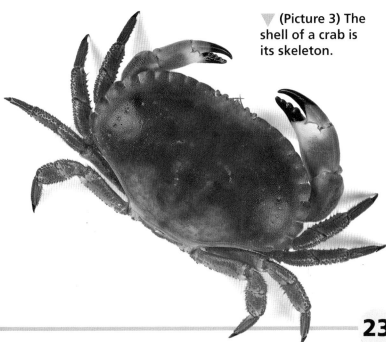

Muscle

Muscle

▲ (Picture 4) Clams and similarly shelled animals are very soft inside. They attach themselves to each of their shells and use their muscles to open and close their shells.

Summary

- Some animals have a watery skeleton.
- Some animals, such as insects, have a hard, outer skeleton.
- To grow, an animal with a hard, outer skeleton has to moult.

Weblink: www.science-at-school.com

Index

Science@School

Science@School is a series published by Atlantic Europe Publishing Company Ltd.

 Atlantic Europe Publishing

Teacher's Guide
There is a Teacher's Guide to accompany this book, available only from the publisher.

CD-ROMs
There are browser-based CD-ROMs containing information to support the series. They are available from the publisher.

Dedicated Web Site
There's more information about other great Science@School packs and a wealth of supporting material available at our dedicated web site:

www.science-at-school.com

First published in 2002 by
Atlantic Europe Publishing Company Ltd

Copyright © 2002
Atlantic Europe Publishing Company Ltd

All rights reserved. No part of this publication may be reproduced, stored in a retrieval system, or transmitted in any form or by any means, electronic, mechanical, photocopying, recording or otherwise, without prior permission of the publisher.

Author
Brian Knapp, BSc, PhD

Educational Consultant
Peter Riley, BSc, C Biol, MI Biol, PGCE

Art Director
Duncan McCrae, BSc

Senior Designer
Adele Humphries, BA, PGCE

Editor
Lisa Magloff, BA

Illustrations
David Woodroffe

Designed and produced by
EARTHSCAPE EDITIONS

Reproduced in Malaysia by
Global Colour

Printed in Hong Kong by
Wing King Tong Company Ltd

Science@School
Volume 4A *Moving and growing*
A CIP record for this book is available from the British Library.

Paperback ISBN 1 86214 124 X

Picture credits
All photographs are from the Earthscape Editions photolibrary.

This product is manufactured from sustainable managed forests. For every tree cut down at least one more is planted.